RIGHT TO OBLIVION

A WAY TO GET TO KNOW OURSELVES AND SHARE THE KNOWLEDGE

J. Aranda Serralbo

June 2012, London, UK

J. Aranda Serralbo
Right to Oblivion, A way to get to know ourselves and
share the knowledge

© 2013, J. Aranda Serralbo
Self publishing
javieraranda@outlook.com

Contents

Acronyms

AMA: American Marketing Association

BBC: British Broadcasting Corporation

CDN: Content Distribution Network

CPC: Cost per Click

CPM: Cost per Mille

CTR: Click through Rate

FTC: Federal Trade Commission

ICO: Information Commissioner's Office

NAI: Network Advertising Initiative

Non-PII: Non Personal Identifiable Information

OBA: Online Behavioural Advertising

PII: Personal Identifiable Information

TACD: Trans Atlantic Consumer Dialog

Acknowledgments

I would like to thank all the people I have been surrounded by throughout the development of this book for all of their support. Undoubtedly, without their comprehension and willingness to talk about privacy and memory, I would not have had the courage to see this project through to the end. To all of them, thank you.

I would also like to thank Dimitrios Tsivrikos for his support given to me since the very first moment I introduced my idea to him until the completion of it. Both his shared enthusiasm as well as his wise advice made this book possible. Merci beaucoup.

And last but not the least, I want to deeply thank my beloved partner for her unconditional support throughout these months of research and hard work. Her vision and her understanding of my way of thinking, together with her advice, has been of great importance in accomplishing this book. To her and all mentioned previously Mil Gracias!

-The existence of forgetting has never been proved: we only know that some things don't come to mind when we want them to.-

Friedrich Nietzsche

Chapter I

Memory and Technology

The human being has evolved with the ability to forget (Damasio, 2010). The human brain is the product of an adaptative process of million of years (Foster, J.K., 2009). The outcome allows us to remember the events of yesterday better than those of last year, and what happened an hour ago even more clearly. We recall the events of our childhood in vivid detail whereas the experiences of two years ago seem impossible to recall.

The more we repeat an experience the easier it is to remember it. In 1890, William James questioned in Principles of Psychology why drugs, fevers, asphyxia and excitement can awaken things that were forgotten a long time ago. He pointed out that discovering the reason *"becomes the psychologist's most interesting task"*. A lot of water has passed under the bridge since then, psychology has moved forward along with other sciences like neuroscience, bringing us closer to uncovering the mysteries of mind (Kesinger et al., 2011; Reyna et al., 2012; Hasson et al., 2012).

Human beings have two kinds of memory: The explicit and implicit memory. The explicit memory is the conscious, intentional recollection of past events and information. We use explicit memory everyday when we try to remember the time of a meeting or when recollecting a birthday years ago. There are two types of explicit memory: (1) episodic memory, this is autobiographical memory consists of the recollection of events in the life of a person and (2) semantic memory which consists of all explicit memory that is not autobiographical like historical events and figures; the ability to recognize friends and acquaintances; and information learned in school, such as specialized vocabularies, reading, writing and mathematics (Tulving, E., 2002). On the other hand, we find the implicit memory, a type of memory in which previous experiences aid in the performance of a task without conscious awareness of these previous experiences (Schacter, D.L., 1987)

If someone asks you to recall what you did on 29th February this year, you would probably have to think hard to provide an answer. If you have a good memory, or a special event took place on that day, you might be able to recall a few events. In contrast, the author can tell you instantly that he did at least 18 things on 29th February (Appendix A). In chronological order, these are the highlights:

- It was the day he learnt how to say *futbolín* in German: fussball

- He read the lyrics of the song 'I Won't Give Up' by Jason Mraz for the first time

- He did research into universities in Barcelona that offer a Phd in Neuroscience

- He learnt the concept of 'clickjacking'

- He decided to watch the film Moonrise Kingdom after watching the trailer

- He found a tennis partner online

- Someone told him about the book 'Social Neuroscience: People Thinking about Thinking People'. He had a look at its index

The author would like to say he has a good memory, unfortunately it's pretty average (Reitz et al., 2009). Luckily, he is not the only one able to enumerate what he did yesterday or 1, 2 or 3 months ago. He can even tell you what he did a year ago!

We are all Internet users who use a browser to connect to the World Wide Web. All browsers have a browsing history which store everything we do online. Bearing in mind that the average user in the United Kingdom spends 35.6 hours per month online (Comscore, 2011) each of us has the possibility to access 427.2 hours, the equivalent of 17.8 days, of information about our experiences and behaviour on the Internet. This number reaches 2 months and 2 days for teenagers (Cybersentinel, 2009).

With the emergence of new technologies and mobiles devices, we are able to generate and store more and more information about our actions online. Arguably, our implicit memory of our online behaviour is taking a turn towards the explicit. By retrieving information in such an easy way, we could be taking one of the most important steps forward in the evolution of memory to date.

The Internet user cannot yet benefit from all the information that he or she generates on a daily basis. Online behaviour still has an implicit nature to us. Nevertheless, every time users go online, they allow companies such as Google to store their data and implicit experiences so that they can offer what the brand has come to call *"one beautifully simple experience"* which *"over time will mean better Google search results and ads"*(Google, 2012). As a result, Internet users are destined to forget their experiences while companies carefully monitor all of this information to offer advertisements that better target the online user. In other words, brands remember what users forget.

Of all the data gathered by Internet companies, there is still one type of information that they are not able to decode: our intentions. Online companies know what users do, but they do not know why they do it. This book will explore the techniques that companies use to predict users' intentions with the goal of offering tailored advertisements.

Internet privacy has generated discord between users and companies in the past few years (Acquisti, 2010). An advertisement technique called Online Behavioural Targeting (OBA) has created controversy in the user community. This book will explain how this technique works and what is used for by Internet companies (Chapter II). Likewise, this paper will clarify the type of companies and organizations involved in managing online user data and how different legislation regulates UK and USA Internet privacy (Chapter III).

Research was carried out into the number of tailored advertisements received by Internet users (Chapter IV). We will discover the huge differences in the amount of tailored advertisements received by an a user who opts-in, sharing his or her data with online companies to receive better offers from brands and a Internet user who opts-out, choosing not to share his or her data. This book will reveal information on the number of Internet companies tracking both types of user online, gathering data in an attempt to better target the user with behavioural advertising.

Online users are becoming more aware of the data economy market. This book will discuss how users, consumers and society in general are finding out how companies and governments are using the data they generate online (Chapter V). This awareness is starting to create a new market in which users are data owners, trading the information they produce every day (Chapter VI).

New trends and advances in technology offer a new opportunity to users, consumers, companies and society as a whole. An idea of how to put together all of the available technology to create a digital memory will be proposed (Chapter VII). This digital memory would help everyone to get to know themselves better through the analysis and measurement of their own behaviour and to share it for the benefit of society.

This book will attempt to clarify how to improve the relationship between companies and Internet users who decide to share their online behaviour. A way of creating a truly unique relationship between consumers and brands online will be suggested (Chapter VIII). This is a relationship in which the Internet user is the owner of the data on their online actions, a bond which would be mutually beneficial to both brands and consumers.

Chapter II

Satisfying Consumers

It may seem strange to say it, but it is worth reminding companies that there is no business without clients. In every market, products must appeal to clients' emotional wants and needs. In order to survive, every company needs to know the preferences of its clients to offer them what they need. As Kotler and Gary Armstrong rightly stated in Principles of Marketing in 1996:

"The goal of marketing is to create customer satisfaction profitably by building value-laden relationships with important customers."

To do so requires a process of communication between the company and the client. While this process has changed throughout the years, the goal has always been to maintain a relationship between the company and the client that allows the former to be profitable. The way companies have decided what to offer is established by the analysis and gathering of data. It is in this process that marketing has gained an important role.

Marketing is an applicable science that attempts to explain and influence how companies and consumers behave. Marketing models are usually applications of economic theories. *These theories are of general application and produce precise predictions, based on strong and rational supposition about companies and consumers* (Ho & Camerer, 2006).

Behavioural Targeting

Marketing is defined by the American Marketing Association (AMA, 2007) as:

"The activity, set of institutions, and processes for creating, communicating, delivering, and exchanging offerings that have value for customers, clients, partners, and society at large."

To achieve this goal of offering value to customers, companies have put into practice countless marketing techniques. These range from customers satisfaction surveys, focus groups, loyalty cards to customer panels and CRM. The latest technique, which allows companies to gather information about customers, is Behavioural Targeting.

Behavioural Targeting is what many marketers call the *"Holy Grail"* of marketing (Chen & Stallaert, 2010). Nowadays, there are companies on the Internet that can gather real-time information about users as they browse. Companies send cookies, a piece of text that a web server can store on a user's every time they connect to the Internet, identifying each user individually. This allows companies to track a user's online behaviour. The system has been developed to offer tailored advertisements to users based on the information companies store about them. This is a real-time relationship between company and the consumer.

Among the different kinds of Behavioural Targeting we find Online Behavioural Advertising (OBA). This model is used by Ad Networks to show advertisements to Internet users depending on their online behaviour. The aim is to show the right advertisement to the right user. To do so, Ad Networks analyses the information they gather from each user to be able to show them the most tailored advertisements possible.

How does OBA work?

To put it simply, OBA is similar to the experience any user could have with an e-tailer. For instance, Amazon has created a profile of each user's searches and purchases. Users are prompted with products that could be of interest according to their previous purchasing behaviour (Yan et al., 2009). The difference between Behavioural Targeting within the Amazon website and OBA is that OBA tracks the users everywhere online whilst Amazon only tracks the user on its website. In the case of OBA, the Internet becomes a sort of endless shopping experience, in which the user is prompted with products that he or she might be interested in according to past behaviour.

All of a user's interests and our online behaviour end up becoming part of a database stored by Ad Networks and tracking companies. The business of Ad Networks is to create advertising campaigns. They are in constant contact with publishers and brands to ensure that these campaigns succeed.

The two most common ways of measuring the performance of advertisements are: Impressions, the number of times an advertisement is displayed to an online user measured per 1000 views (CPM) or by clicks, the number of times a user clicks on an advertisement measured by 'Click Through Rate' (CTR). For an Ad Network, it is easy to keep count of the number of impressions or clicks per advertisement, the difficult part is reaching the right target audience.

Taking Google as an example, to open a gmail account a user must provide demographic information when registering the account, such as age, gender and location. These are the minimum details needed to register an email account. If Google then has a campaign based on impressions or clicks for men and women aged between 35-45 and living in the UK, if the demographic details of the user match with the desired audience of the campaign, he or she may be selected as possible target. Companies do not always rely on the information given by the users. The reliability of the demographic information provided is questionable. A user may give false information or elements of his or her information may change, such as location, without the knowledge of the email provider. How do companies find the right target if the information provided by the users if not up-to-date or reliable?

Ad Networks are able to improve the probability that a user will be the right target for an advertisement. Let's think about a campaign based on the performance of CTR (Click Through Rate). If an Internet user clicks on an advertisement, he or she becomes into successful target. The algorithm's goal will be to find the same behaviour in the data of other users. The algorithm assumes that users with similar online behaviour would be likely to click on the same type of advertisments. In other words, users that click on advertismentss tell the algorithm that users with their behaviour profile would increase the CTR (**Chen et al., 2009; Benevenuto et al., 2009**)

Companies do not need to know who the user is to know that he or she could be the right target. These models are implemented out of million of terabytes of data and some of them are able to create 450 in one day (Chen et al., 2009). The models get improve as users browse on the internet and click on ads.

Online Behavioural Targeting has been proven to improve the CTR of a campaign by 670% (Yan et al., 2009). Regardless of whether a campaign is based on impressions or on clicks or whether users click on an advertisement or not, just by being online every user is participating in enhancing the performance of OBA.

The mathematical algorithm behind OBA is not able to predict why user clicks on advertisements. The method it uses to predict intention is content. Companies such as Google have a content taxonomy (Toubiana et al., 2010; list Content Taxonomy Appendix B). Every time users use Google search, Google classifies the search according to a content. The same happens when users visits different websites. Each website is classified according to a theme. When a user has visited a website, he or she receives a cookie. These cookies are stored in the user's computer and analyzed by the corresponding Ad Network before the user is shown one or another advertisement.

The process of analysis takes place in milliseconds and the analysis matches the user with the most fitting advertisement according to their behaviour. Likewise, the advertisements are placed usually before the web page content due to they are served from a content distribution network (CDN) which has servers close to the users (Toubiana et al., 2010). This makes the uploading of the advertisements a smooth process that passes unnoticed by the user.

The experience of OBA is defended by companies such as Google as positive. Companies say they want to offer users a unique experience and that the more a consumer uses their tool the better and the more unique the experience will be (Google, 2012). Not only will a user's online experience be improved as he or she browses and searches but the advertisements the user sees will be tailored to him or her.

This kind of unique experiences has generated complaints from many different users. For example, Amazon was sued for showing different prices for the same products to different users (Acquisti, 2010) suffering what could arguably be described as significant PR damage. Consumers are likely to view the use of their data in ways that may result in higher prices as unacceptable and intrusive. This technique is what is called Online Targeting *of Prices,* normally used to categorise customers according to their postcode or country of residence with the purpose of showing them discount and vouchers according to their online behaviour (Office of Fair Trading, 2010).

All of this is targeting is possible thanks to the cookies that are sent to and stored by users' computers. While users navigate the Internet, the web or server analyses these cookies in order to personalize the users' experience. These techniques have caused concern among users and contributed to new government regulation in the UK and the USA on online privacy.

Chapter III

Privacy

From the very first moment a user connects to the Internet, bytes of information are generated about his or her behaviour. This information has been managed by companies for over 12 years, companies whose core business is online advertising. The following research shows which organizations, companies and institutions are gathering the information generated by users online.

There are 3 parties involved in every online advertisement:

Advertiser a party that has an online advertisement that it wants to embed in web pages across the Internet. The advertiser is willing to pay for this service.

Publisher a party that owns a web page (or web site) and is willing to place advertisements from others on its pages. The publisher expects to be paid for this service.

Ad Networks a party that collects advertisements (and payment) from advertisers and places them on publishers pages (along with paying the publishers). Examples of Ad Networks are Google, Yahoo!, MSN and AOL.

The goal of these companies is to tailor advertisements to the user so that they can see them, click on them to buy the product advertised or subscribe to the website or blog.

The way to improve the likelihood of users clicking on an advertisement, or to find out if the advertisement is being seen by the desired target, is through data gathering about the user and his or her behaviour. This analysis and data gathering has been regulated throughout the years.

Behavioural targeting divides browsing information into Personally Identifiable Information (PII) and non Personally Identifiable Information (non-PII). Categories of PII include name, email address and social security number. Non-PII is basically everything else about the user, including age, gender, ethnicity, the websites he or she visits and the pages he or she views. The collection of non-PII is carried out by many e-commerce sites without explicit consent from the consumer. It is the objective of behavioural targeting to collect non-PII.

In 1999, a group of companies started engaging with OBA. OBA is a form of advertising in which advertising networks construct profile of users as they navigate different websites (Dixon, 2007). These companies were trying to improve the efficiency of their services by gathering huge amounts of data from users.

This group of companies created the Network Advertising Initiative (NAI) and they submitted their principles to The American Federal Trade Commission (FTC) in 1999. The FTC asked them to start regulating their activities, recommending a basic level of privacy protection. In 2001, the NAI produced a document of their principles, a document that was reviewed in 2008. Nowadays, 90 companies are members of the NAI, out of 227 companies in the business of data collection listed by some sources in USA (Abine, online privacy company, 2012). Urged by the FTC, the NAI began to offer an opt-out button that enable consumers to prevent behavioural advertisements being shown to them. This is only effective on behavioural advertising by members of the NAI. As there are just 90 companies that belong to the organization and this regulation is not mandatory, the user cannot opt-out entirely of behavioural advertisements.

In 2009, the EU issued a directive banning the use of cookies without prior consent. The directive was not a law but forced the members states to create their own law. This was due by May 2011, only 3 of the 27 countries within the EU met the deadline: Denmark, Estonia and the UK. The UK, through the Information Commissioner's Office (ICO) then realised the market wasn't ready for this directive and gave the industry a year to prepare for the so-called 'Cookie Law'. Starting from May 26th 2012, all website based in the UK will have give the user the option to opt-in.

The Trans Atlantic Consumer Dialog (TACD) is a forum of US and EU consumer organisations which develop and agree on joint consumer policy recommendations for the US government and the European Union. The aim is to promote consumer interest in EU and US policy making. The TACD is trying to introduce the online privacy legislation that is emerging in EU to the USA.

The current situation concerning online privacy in the US and UK are quite different. While the US Senate wants to write new laws to give the FTC *"the power to enforce them with civil penalties which would promote Internet commerce by increasing the trust that Americans put in online transactions"* (New York Times, 9th May 2012), from 26th of May 2012 UK websites will be obligated to offer the user an opt-in option.

Two countries, two different regulations, two different approaches to the same matter. The privacy of Internet users is protected in different ways in different countries, while the World Wide Web has no borders.

Chapter IV

Research

Introduction

The following research aims to analyse the differences between two different types of online browsing style. One in which the user 'opts-in' willingly shares his or her information with companies and third parties, allowing themselves to be tracked, and another in which the user 'opts-out' disabling every available tracking option to prevent companies and third parties from accessing his or her data.

The objective of this research is to investigate the number of companies tracking each type of user as they navigate the Internet. Likewise, the research will record the numbers of advertisements shown to both types of user on each website.

Carrying out the research will reveal the number of companies that access user's data without them being aware of it.

To the best of the author's understanding this is the first research of this kind carried out to show the number of companies tracking users as well as the number of adverisements each user is exposed to while online with the opt-out and opt-in options enabled.

Methodology used

In order to carry out the research, two identical computers (HP Compaq TC 1100) with the same technical characteristics were used. The latest version of Google Chrome *18.0.1025.168 m* was installed on both computers.

Another computer was used to create two gmail accounts:

my.behavior.opting.in@gmail.com
my.behavior.opting.out@gmail.com

Both accounts were registered with the same profile: Gender: Male; Age: 27 and Country: U.K.

The first time Google Chrome was launched on each computer, the email addresses were set up in the browser, one per computer.

To be able to identify the companies tracking each user, the computers were installed with the software Do Not Track Plus from the company Abine (http://abine.com)

"Do Not Track Plus blocks web beacons and other tracking technologies that advertisers use to track user browsing behaviour. It allows users to easily see what trackers are in use at each website an user visit and block any or all of them"

The program identifies tracking companies and advertisers and classifies them into three groups: (1) Social Networks, Ad Networks and (3) Companies tracking you. Every time a user enters a web page, the program is able to identify the number of companies that are trying to access the user's information. The user can block or allow companies to access their data.

To carry out the research, 100 blogs, the top 5 blogs per category in 20 categories, were selected from the website Blog Rank (http://www.invesp.com/blog-rank). Blog Rank rates blogs according to number of unique visitors.

BlogRank is a comprehensive system that collects data on thousands of blogs, and ranks them in different categories based on over 20 different factors.

A list with 100 blogs was generated in Excel. The blogs were divided in 20 categories within nine sectors:

- **Art & Literature:** Music, Photography, Art
- **Business**: Finance, Business
- **Computer**: Blogging, Social Media
- **Health**
- **Interests**: Shopping, Autos, Beauty, Humour, Fashion, Movies
- **Life & People:** Dating, Sex, Life, Parenting
- **Sports**
- **Travel**

Both the opt-in and the opt-out users were sent an email containing this list of blogs. Both users visited the landing page of each blog listed. Neither clicked on any online advertisement or entered the sites beyond the landing page. Neither of the computers was used to visit any site which was not included in the list of blogs.

Simultaneously, the number of companies tracking each user and the number of advertisements viewed by each was recorded.

The advertisements selected for the study were classified into two types:

Standard advertisements: any advertisement promoting the blog itself or by blog sponsors

Ad Choices: Online Behavioural Advertisements, these are identifiable by the Ad Choices Logo each bears.

Findings

The number of companies tracking the opt-out user in comparison to the number tracking the opt-in user was very revealing (Table 4.1). While the user who opted-out was not tracked throughout the browsing experience at any time, the user who opted-in was tracked on every blog but one. The opt-in user was tracked by up to 31 companies per blog.

Number of companies tracking user	Opt-in	Opt-out
[0]	1	100
[1-5]	11	0
[6-10]	27	0
[11-15]	32	0
[16-20]	10	0
[21-25]	12	0
[26-30]	6	0
[31+]	1	0
total blogs	100	100

Table 4.1

The opt-in user was tracked 1307 times in total with an average of 13.1 companies tracking his online experience as he browsed through the blogs (Table 4.2).

Tracking company type	Number of times the user was tracked
Social Networks	107
Ad Networks	506
Tracking Companies	694
Total	1307
Average number of tracking companies per blog	13.1

Table 4.2

The opt-out user was shown 55 advertisements over 100 blogs while the opt-in user was shown nearly six times as many, 292 in total. Of the advertisements seen by the opt-in user, 187 were normal advertisements and 105 were Ad Choices advertisements (Table 4.3). This means that the opt-out user was exposed to over 80% less advertisements than the opt-in user.

Advertisement Type	Number viewed by the opt-in user	Number viewed by the opt –out user
Standard advertisements	187	55
Average number of normal advertisements shown	1.87	0.55
Ad Choices	105	0
Average number of ad choices advertisments shown	1.5	0
Total	292	55
Average number of advertisements per blog	**2.92**	**0.55**

Table 4.3

The blog sector within which the opt-in user was tracked the most was 'Life & People', being tracked 287 times in total (Table 4.4). The sector in which the opt-in user was tracked the least was 'Health', being tracked just 37 times.

Category	% of total number of tracking companies	Number of tracker companies	Unique blog users per month
Life	8.80	115	1,570,994
Parenting	6.50	85	6,848,075
Social Media	6.43	84	3,806,006
Autos	6.27	82	3,779,004
Sports	6.04	79	145,047
Finance	5.97	78	6,169,438
Humour	5.81	76	7,412,011
Shopping	5.66	74	454,170
Movies	5.51	72	4,431,117
Fashion	4.74	62	1,957,205
Music	4.74	62	3,094,480
Blogging	4.59	60	528,125
Art	4.51	59	567,453
Beauty	4.28	56	7,160,725
Business	3.75	49	62,792,835
Travel	3.75	49	1,206,051
Dating	3.52	46	1,203,292
Photography	3.14	41	582,711
Sex	3.14	41	129,557
Health	2.83	37	1,114,777
Total	**100**	**1307**	**114,953,073**

Table 4.4

According to the research, Facebook was the Social Network that tracked the opt-in user the most, tracking the user on 67% of all the pages visited. The *Dedicated Networks* was the Ad Network that tracked the opt-in user the most, on 82 out of 100 blogs. The tracking company which tracked the user most was Google Analytics, in 88% of the blogs visited (Table 4.5).

Tracking company Type	% of blogs tracked	Name of company
Social Networks	67	Facebook
	40	Twitter
Ad Networks	82	Dedicated Networks
	63	Quantcast
Tracking Companies	88	Google Analytics
	79	Double Click
	64	Comscore Beacon
	64	Quantcast
	54	Google Adsense

Table 4.5

Based on the information gathered about the number of advertisements per blog and because all of the blogs selected featured information on their number of monthly users, it was possible to estimate the potential revenue of each website for Cost Per Mille (CPM) and Cost Per Click (CPC).

To estimate the potential annual revenue of each blog, the Hochman Consultants (Hochman, 2011) estimation for the 2011 CPC, CPM and CTR was used. The dollar value was converted into pounds with a currency value of 0.62 pounds per dollar (Appendix C).Table 6 shows the analysis carried out based on the consultancy's estimation and the research carried out in this study.

It shows that in the case of all users opting-out of the 100 blogs featured, the potential annual loss for these blogs would be £10,709,184.60 of their potential revenue from CPM. If all users opted-out, the potential annual loss from the CPC revenue would be of £112,141.71 (for the estimation a CTR of 0.4% was applied) Table 4.6.

	Monthly users of the 100 blogs featured in this research	114,953,073
	Potential Annual Users of these Blogs	1,379,436,876
OPT-IN	**Total Advertisements**	294
OPT-OUT	**ADVERTISEMENTS**	55
Potential Annual Revenue	**CPM £2,46**	£12,759,538.44
OPT-IN	**CPC £0,644 (CTR 0.4%)**	£133,612.08
Potential Annual Revenue	**CPM £2,46**	£2,050,353.84
OPT-OUT	**CPC £0,644 (CTR 4%)**	£21,470.37
Potential Revenue Loss OPT-OUT	**CPM**	**£10,709,184.60**
	CPC	**£112,141.71**

Table 4.6

Discussion

The research has shown the difference between two styles of browsing: one in which the user shares his data with companies by opting-in and another in which the user prevented companies from accessing his data by opting-out. The results show that while the user who opted-out wasn't tracked by any companies, an average of 13.1 tracked the user who opted-in.

The data gathered showed how it is not necessary to have long established Internet account to be tracked. From the very first page visited by the newly created opt-in user, companies were tracking his online behavoiur. This user was tracked by 1307 companies without being asked at any time for permission to access his data.

The difference in the number of advertiments shown to each user was very significant. A total of 292 advertisements were viewed by the opt-in user while the opt-out user was shown over 80% less, just 55 advertisements. Of these, 187 viewed by the opt-in user and all of those viewed by the opt-out user were standard advertisements.

Almost 71% (132) of the standard advertisements shown to the opt-in user were gathering some kind of information from his computer. These did not have the Ad Choices Logo so the law does not class them as online behavioural advertisements. However, according to this research, they accessed and tracked the user's data. As they do not feature the Ad Choices Logo, this tracking was unbeknown to the user. These advertisements were not viewed by the opt-out user.

The nature of these advertisements is not clear, but the research indicates that Ad Networks need to read or send some sort of information to the user's computer to be able show the advertisement. For instance, this data could allow Ad Networks to show advertisements to the user that they haven't been shown before, or to show an advert a specific number of times, or just a simple way of keeping track of the Impressions.

Almost 36% of the advertisements shown to the opt-in user were identifiable by a logo as Ad Choices advertisments. This means that a total of 105 advertisements were shown based on the behaviour of the user. While we are not aware of the exact process used by the algorithim of these advertisments, it is clear that the user does not need to have an email account for a long time to be targeted by behavioural advertisements.

The value of the online advertisement market hit £19.6 billion in 2011 (Computer World UK, April 2012). The estimation for the potential revenue loss in this research shows a big difference in revenue generated between an opt-in and an opt-out browsing style. While blogs owners, in this case, and advertising companies are potentially able to make a lot of money from advertisements, the user is enabling this revenue but not participating in the profit. The benefit delivered to the user is a personalised experience through tailored advertisements.

Future Research

Further research is recommended to highlight the number of companies tracking users while they browse as well as the nature of the advertisements they are shown. The purpose would be to inform the user about what is happening with the data they generate online and why their data is being used in this way.

Chapter V

Privacy Awareness

It has been difficult for Internet users to understand the terms and conditions contracted with Internet companies when signing up to any of their services (Stevens, 2011). One of the requirements imposed by the Federal Trade Commission on companies is the implementation of the opt-out button. This is designed to make it easier and clearer for users to understand what it means to share their data with companies. Research has pointed out that if all of the Internet users in the USA were to read the terms and conditions when signing up to create an email account, the country would lose $781 billion due to the time that would take them to read the entire document (McDonald & Cranor, 2008).

While working on this book, the situation for Internet companies has been in a state of flux. Likewise, 8 days after this book is completed, the Cookie Law is going to implement a revolutionary change that will have a huge impact on the Internet experience for UK users. On 26th May 2012 all UK websites must offer users opt-in consent tools to allow cookies that pass information about users' browsing activities to third parties. The law facilitates software called Optanon to make the website compliant (http://www.cookielaw.org). If companies fail to do so, the ICO can fine website owners up to £500k (Talk business Magazine, April 2012).

Without yet knowing how this will affect the market, 82% of digital marketers think the EU cookie law is bad for the Web (EU e-Privacy Directive Survey, March 2012). UK businesses seem to be against the law due the cost of adapting to it. Businesses claim they could lose £10 billion due to a combination of lost sales, damage to existing technology and advertising businesses as a result of the law (The Telegraph, April 2012).

Internet users are experiencing a learning process regarding privacy. Since 2002, surveys show an increasing concern about how users are being tracked and how companies use the collected data (Paine Schofield et al., 2007; Anton et al., 2010). According to the EU e-Privacy Directive survey (March 2012), 89% of UK consumers think that the EU Cookie Law is a positive step and 79% agreed that the changes were needed due to the lack of public knowledge about cookies. Interestingly, 23% of respondents were happy for websites to use cookies to improve their browsing experience, which is the same number who said that they would be keen to opt-in.

Increasingly, Internet privacy laws are being featured in the Press, causing growing concern among consumers. A glimpse at headlines over the last five months illustrates this situation:

January 2012
— European Commission to reveal plans to change data privacy laws, *BBC*
— The battle over your data, *BBC*
— Could Google's data hoarding be good for you? *BBC*

February 2012

- Obama Turns to Web Industry for Consumer Privacy Standard, *Bloomberg News*
- The Consumer Privacy Bill of Rights: Are We the Consumers, Or Are We the Product? *Businessweek*
- The end of online privacy? *The Guardian*

March 2012

- Google is now just an ad company': Departing exec's Goldman Sachs-style rant about how search giant is now obsessed with harvesting people's private information, *Dailymail*
- Stealing your privacy -- it's Google once again, *Fox News*
- Yahoo says it will implement do-not-track worldwide later this year, *PC Advisor*
- Privacy and the power of Google, *The Guardian*
- Google privacy changes 'in breach of EU law', *BBC*

April 2012

- Your Privacy Is Tested With Every Click You Make, *New York Times*
- Tim Berners-Lee: demand your data from Google and Facebook, *The Guardian*
- Facebook's $100bn privacy dilemma, *The Guardian*
- European Regulator Warns Silicon Valley About Privacy, *New York Times*

May 2012

- New 'cookies' rule looms, *Financial Times*
- Giving up our liberty for free, one click at a time, *The Telegraph*
- 9 May, 2012: F.T.C. and White House Push for Online Privacy Laws, *New York Times*

The press coverage of Internet Privacy has brought the issue home to consumers on a daily basis, creating debate within the Internet community.

Another reason why the privacy issue has become public knowledge is because the U.S. House of Representatives has recently passed the Cyber Intelligence Sharing and Protection Act (CISPA). Passed this April, the stated aim of the bill is to help the U.S. Government investigate cyber threats and ensure the security of networks against cyber attack (House Rules Committee, April 2012). The news that the bill had been approved sparked worldwide controversy, causing consumer concern that the bill would spread to other countries and erradicate users' online privacy. The new bill would allow the government, in cases approved by the American Senate, to access web users' private data on suspicion of a cyber threat. It would also allow easier information-sharing between security agencies and private web firms like Google or Facebook (BBC, April 2012).

It is interesting to analyse how two different governments have approached the same issue in contrasting ways. While the ICO will implement the CookieLaw on 26th May, fining websites owners with up to £500k if they do not comply; the equivalent organisation in the United States offered Internet companies the opportunity to self regulate. The UK opted to protect Internet users by law:

"All UK websites must offer users opt-in consent tools to allow cookies that pass information about your browsing activities to 3rd parties."

While the USA government left data protection regulation in the hands of companies. The self-regulated NAI created an opt-out button and claimed:

"The NAI Opt-out Tool was developed in conjunction with our members for the express purpose of allowing consumers to "opt out" of the Behavioural advertising delivered by our member companies."

The NAI claimed in their 2011 Compliance review that after implementing the opt-out button they received 6 million unique visitors and of these, 840,000 in total. That represents an opt-out rate of 14%. This raises the question of whether the Cookie Law will have the reverse effect. Now that the user has the option to opt-in rather than to opt-out, will a similarly low percentage choose to do so? The latest research forecasts that 23% of users would chose to opt-in, according to the EU e-Privacy Directive survey (March 2012).

Only time will tell whether or not American consumers will eventually demand the data protection rights of UK users or if, on the contrary, UK Internet users would prefer the American way. Only the passing of time will clarify the situation, but if there is something that every company should consider in the current climate, it's a new business model clarifying how and why they are gathering information from users.

Chapter VI

Data as Commodity

The research shows the number of companies that follow Internet users is very high. Internet users are increasingly aware that their digital data has a value and a price and they want their cut of the profits (Kennedy, 2011). This power struggle over the control of personal data is transforming today's customers from passive to active market participants. They now have more power than even the largest multinational brands. As David Siegel, author of "Pull: The Power of the Semantic Web to Transform Your Business", wrote on his blog:

"Once you are in control of your own behaviour, purchasing, viewing and other data, you will be able to trade it for offers, discounts and even cash rebates on various products and services".

Once the user's rights have been protected, data comes at a price. A January 2011 survey of 900 people across five countries by firm Frog Design monitored how much consumers were willing to pay to protect their personal data. Demographic information, contact details and social profiling data such as hobbies and interests were deemed to be worth less than $5 a year. Physical location history was worth $55 annually, while web search history was valued at $57 a year. (Appendix D). This raises the question, are users prepared to do business with their data?

Polls say that 84% of people from the UK would sell their data in exchange for money or coupons (May 2012). There are already a number of companies that offer the possibility of managing personal data in exchange for something of value.

Personal.com: offers users the possibility of storing personal data by theme. Users can store their data with Personal.com and they have the opportunity to sell it to companies to earn more than $1,000 a year.

"Use your power to demand that companies play by a fair and transparent set of rules if they want to access your data".

Personal.com enables individuals to own, control, access and benefit from their online personal information. The start-up's aim is to disrupt the online business model. (Washintong Post, 2011)

Similarly, i-Allow.com enables users to opt-out of junk marketing and protects their information by providing a controlled approach to data sharing.

"We can then help you use your data to get value, for example by anonymously matching what you want to buy to personalise offers from the leading brands".

i-Allow.com empowers its users by giving them control of how their data is used. According to Basini i-Allow's CEO:

"Only 10% of the members choose not to share their data with anybody. The other 90% self-select into a range of different attitudes, from 'I like sharing my data with brands that I like, and I want to receive relevant contact from those brands with my permission' to 'I do not care where my data goes as long as I get a cut of the action. About 30% take the latter option".

This is partly because i-Allow.com rewards those who offer their data to marketers and advertisers with cash. *"The reason we went for cash, rather than free socks, or vouchers, is that cash is a very powerful motivator,"* says Basini. *"One of the things the market needs to do is to provide these very clear incentive mechanisms, so that the consumer understands the value exchange that is going on."* (Research, 2011)

Blurum.it: *'straights to the points'* Blurum offers users the opportunity to exchange their data for points. The user can also exchange accrued point to exchange them for products.

Absolute Radio: Consumers are also sharing their location information in exchange for offers or improved services. UK radio station Absolute Radio has introduced targeted in-stream advertising for listeners using the Internet or smartphone apps. 'Smart Streamers' who sign-in using Facebook,   receive advertisements targeted to their location in exchange for a higher-quality audio feed. The station also plans to enable loyal listeners to replace advertising breaks with songs of their choice in exchange for regular listening.

O2: Mobile phone company O2's Priority Moments scheme, launched in July 2011, provides money-off coupons and offers from brands based on the user's location. O2 has teamed up with brands including WH Smith, Harvey Nichols, Zizzi, Odeon, Hotel Chocolat, French Connection and Fitness Firs for the scheme.

Reputation.com: There is also a category of companies like Reputation.com which tries to help people remove or correct private information that appears about them online, with prices starting at a few pounds a month.

The data business creates a need for storage. In the future, the amount of information generated by each user will be increased exponentially as users will remain connected to the Internet at all times (European Commission, 2009). All this information will have to be stored. It is forecasted that data banks will become a £1bn business in the future (Information Age, 2012).

We should stop and think about data not just as a business but also as a source of information. Whether big companies such as Google are the ones storing users' data or it is small companies offering different data management solutions, we will inevitably generate a huge amount of data. Ultimately, this will mean that data exists about every individual's behaviour and on the behaviour of society as a whole. The next chapter will analyze the opportunities that storing information on user behaviour could have, not only for companies but for society itself.

Chapter VII

Digital Memory

The original aim of this book was to compare the different experiences users have on the Internet by showing the abuse of their personal data. All of the discoveries made during the investigation process, as well as the turn of events in the media since the beginning of the year, demonstrate that Internet privacy is in a state of transition.

The era of Internet companies accessing user data without their knowledge or consent is coming to an end. The forthcoming CookieLaw which enforce every website in the UK to offer users opt-in consent tools is evidence of this.

This book proposes an idea of how people, as well as companies, can benefit from the tracking of personal data. An idea that could be of benefit to everyone: users, companies and above all society. In the Information Age, a new type of memory is possible. A memory that stores not only all of the information generated by users manually but also all of the information generated from our behaviour. We need a Digital Memory. The author calls it Oblivion.

When everything is out there

The current trends, technologies and research that make this idea possible are:

Self awareness [Know thyself]

There is growing interest in self-awareness. An increasing number of people call themselves self quantifiers (http://quantifiedself.com). More and more groups of Internet users are interested in improving themselves and their self-knowledge through self-tracking. To do so, they are using technology.

The philosophy of Kaizen, the Japanese term for continuous improvement or change for the better, is beginning to reach a wider population of users as tracking technologies become more accessible. Research shows that '20% of UK adults have used apps or websites to track their health. Among 18 to 34 year-olds, this rises to 36%' (Kennedy, 2011)

There are a growing number of apps, technologies and websites that are helping these self quantifiers to better track their behaviour:

Jawbone's UP Bracelet: Mobile technology company Jawbone has created a wristband and app called UP, a total health-monitoring device. The app tracks how much a person wearing the bracelet moves, what exercise they do, what and when they eat, as well as how well they are sleeping.

The wristband synchronises with the user's iPhone and transfers data to the app. UP encourages rest by tracking periods of deep and light sleep, promotes healthy eating by taking pictures of the food the user eats and when and sets targets for movement and exercise. (http://jawbone.com/up)

The Zeo Personal Sleep Coach: Zeo headbands measure the users' brainwaves and present graphs each morning of percentages of their light, deep and REM sleep. Self quantifiers can track whether they need to take remedial action in order to get enough restful, restorative sleep. (rhttp://www.myzeo.com/sleep/)

The Withings Body Scale: A WiFi scale for daily use that measures the users lean and fat mass automatically. This allows them to concentrate on the origins of their weight variations.

The web dashboard offers a graphical interface with easy browsing over time and allows users to zoom in on the date ranges of their choice. The WiFi scale can be used by an entire family as the dashboard lets you manage up to 8 users. Adultscan monitor their children's growth directly in the scale's interface so they can keep an eye on their health over time. (http://www.withings.com/en/bodyscale)

The ability to predict and analyze our behaviour

The Human Dynamics Laboratory is a division of the MIT (Massachusetts Institute of Technology) Media Lab that has created a computing platform called Social fMRI. This platform is able to predict people's behaviour based on their media consumption. (http://hd.media.mit.edu/)

49

The platform understands how social patterns spread, and uses algorithms to predict how people adopt trends. In 2011, the MIT Media Lab gave 130 participants a smartphone app that tracked their social interaction, logging phone conversations, text messages and email trails (Wired, 2012)

The Human Dynamics Laboratory claims to have invented the technology of reality mining, which, according to the study, uses data gathered by sensors to extract subtle patterns that predict future human behaviour. They say this predictive pattern begins with 'honest signals' (Sandy Pentland 2008), human behaviour that has evolved from ancient primate signalling mechanisms. These are major factors in human decision making in everything from job interviews to first dates (Sandy Pentland).

By using data from mobile phones, electronic ID badges, or digital media they are able to track these honest signals creating what they call a 'god's eye' view of how people interact and even 'see' the rhythms of interaction for everyone in a city. This allows them to predict the behaviour of a community using the information gathered.

Modelling the Spread of Opinions, Behaviours and Contagious Diseases

According to the MIT Media Lab, all the available information on human behavioural data could revolutionize traditional social sciences.

50

They are carrying out an investigation called 'The Social Evolution Project'. The goal is to model *how 'things' spread through society'*. Their aim is to be able to measure and predict: (1) political opinions and news, (2) the spread of obesity and health-related behaviours, (3) contagious diseases and (4) viral media and music.

They approach this by using *socially* aware mobile phones that capture face-to-face interactions and communication patterns within different types of communities.

Culture

Nowadays there are a number of different projects emerging that are all creating a digital database from both culture and the culture generated on a daily basis on the Internet.

Wikipedia: A free, collaboratively edited and multilingual Internet encyclopedia supported by the non-profit Wikimedia Foundation. Its 21 million articles have been written collaboratively by volunteers around the world. Almost all of its articles can be edited by anyone with access to the site, and it has about 100,000 regularly active contributors. As of May 2012, there are editions of Wikipedia in 285 languages. It has become the largest and most popular general reference work on the Internet, ranking sixth globally among all websites on Alexa and having an estimated 365 million readers worldwide (Wikipedia, 2012)

The Internet Memory Foundation: they claim the Internet is becoming the most important source of information on our society and will be a key resource with which to think about it, now and in the future (http://Internetmemory.org/).

Europeana: enables people to explore the digital resources of Europe's museums, libraries, archives and audio-visual collections (http://www.europeana.eu).

All of these ongoing projects store information about our culture once it has been created. However, they do not gather information about the process behind the creation of this culture. There is not yet a process that comprises of the interaction between individuals and their experiences.

The biological anthropologist W.C McGrew suggested in 1998 that we should study culture as a process. He defines this process in 6 steps:

1. A new pattern of behaviour is invented, or an existing one is modified.

2. The innovator transmits this pattern to another.

3. The form of the pattern is consistent within and across performers, perhaps even in terms of recognizable stylistic features.

4. The one who acquires the pattern retains the ability to perform it long after having acquired it.

5. The pattern spreads across social units in a population. These social units may be families, clans, troops, or bands.

6.   The pattern endures across generations.

Why should anthropologists, sociologists, psychologists, individuals and even marketers keep tracking peoples' behaviour when this behaviour is already automatically being tracked every time we connect to the Internet? It is time to start gathering data about ourselves to store it and share it with the world.

A Window to the Future: Oblivion

At the beginning of the twenty first century, we often heard that we were entering the 'Information Age' (David S. Alberts, 2001). The amount of time spent online has increased exponentially during the last decade (Harris Interactive, 2009). Everyone has been immersed in the unprecedented amount of information we have access to. However, it seems that no one has tried to control all of the information generated by our behaviour while accessing this information. Internet companies are an exception, they were using this data to create tailored adverisements. Nowadays we are generating huge amount of information every year (European Commission, 2009), web users created 900 exabytes of personal information in 2010. To put this in perspective 1 exabyte is 1.000.000.000 gigabytes.

We live an age where everything we do online is stored and gathered on a daily basis by the computer, mobile or tablet we use. Never before in history have we had the possibility to have a personal anthropologist and sociologist. A device who observes what we do every day, who take notes of what we do, when we do it, how we do it and who we do things with.

In the era in which anthropologists discuss whether or not non-human primates have culture and in which Internet organizations and marketing companies seek to find the best way of analyzing user behaviour to sell them tailored advertisements, we could be facing an opportunity to find out how our culture is generated so that we can analyse it, study it and store it.

Imagine a Wikipedia of human behaviour where we could store our daily actions. A place where we would have access, not only to our behaviour, but to the behaviour of our family, our friends and even society as a whole. A place where we would be able to have anonymous access to the insights obtained from the analysis of groups, cities, countries and the whole world. Imagine being able to transmit your behaviour to future generations, so they can analyse and learn from previous and current societies. Imagine being able to predict your future behaviour or that of other people thanks to data of millions of people. Imagine that nothing is forgotten and everything remains stored. Welcome to Oblivion.

Oblivion could be the place that would allow us to keep a profile of our behaviour throughout our lifespan. By being able to analyse it, share it and compare it with others, we will develop more awareness of ourselves as individuals, society and therefore as species.

Everyday terabytes of data about our behaviour are generated and, as users, we do not take advantage of them. Everyday, we connect to devices that enable us to interact online. These devices generate data as we use them. Oblivion would be a platform where we would send data about our own activity using different applications on the Internet. This would create a unique user profile for each user.

Oblivion would become a public data bank that would identify patterns of social behaviour among all the information gathered from users. Each user would be able to access their individual information history classified by different themes depending on their activity. Users could obtain insights about their behaviour both individually and combined with other users.

Users could decide at anytime who to share their information with: friends, family or companies. They would be able to sell their data with the latter in the 'behaviour data market'.

Let's think for a moment about what could we do by storing and analyzing our data, for example our location:

Self Awareness: users' profiles would show them data about their everyday journeys. Users could find out which routes they use most and the average time these routes take. They could see the places they have explored in different cities and the ones they have left to explore. This would be built upon throughout users' lives, they could see how their mental map (Frith, 2007) evolves over time. On a family level, by sharing their movements a user could see which part of the world their families have visited in their lives to create a world map of their trips.

Prediction: users would be able to analyse social relationships based on locations within a city or country, gathering information about how friendship and social groups are created in relation to distance. Lack of movement in certain places in the city compared with other data on violence could indicate the need to increase security in the area or a need to improve urban areas. When organizing events, it could give insights into how people move around the city so evacuation systems could be improved.

Cultural: by comparing their profile with others, users could see the places that have been visited more by locals or tourists within a city in a day, year or a decade. They could observe the migration of societies throughout history, allowing them to analyse how different events affect migratory movements.

Social: users could share their movements within a city with their friends, from sharing routes in their home city to offering guidance on other cities they have been to.

Business: by sharing data on users movements with companies and combining it with their consumption behaviour, companies would be able to analyse consumer types by area. This would allow them to sell their products in areas with high numbers of consumers they want to target or to place ads according to the consumers in the area. Video screen and real time data analysis would allow advertisements to change everyday depending on consumers' movements, as happens nowadays on the Internet with OBA. Travel agents could offer tailored trip promotions to consumers on places they haven't visited yet. Restaurants could offer special

56

vouchers to consumers in the area. Real estate companies could define the prices of houses depending on the profile of the neighbours. Knowing where their consumers and potential consumers are would allow companies limitless options to reach them.

With the smartphone and app boom the potential of data collection and analysis has rocketed. There are apps for very different purposes: location, finances, health, education, photography, writing, social networks, etc. Oblivion would be a place where each user could create their own profile, storing their information created online and through apps. This is information that we generate without any cost to ourselves and that in the past was wasted because we did not have access to it.

A digital memory about our behaviour would allow us to get to know ourselves better and sharing it with everyone would allow us to know our society better today and in the future. This would be a small individual contribution to culture that never would be forgotten but remembered in the eternal Oblivion.

Chapter VIII

A new relationship

Internet advertising will improve its efficiency thanks to the opt-in option. Companies are going to improve their relationships with consumers as they will have a better understanding of consumer interests. If the OBA (Online Behavioural Advertising) increased CTR by 670%, OBA with an opt-in option would increase this even more by gathering more reliable data from consumers. As a result, companies will be able to offer customers products they like and predict what they might like more accurately.

A personalized, predictive online marketing tool is emerging. Our interests and behaviour will be analyzed together with the data of other users with similar interests and behaviour. Advertising of the future will show us our next purchase before we even know it. (Target, 2012)

As this happens, the relationship between brand and consumer will evolve over time, becoming more like a friendship. Wikipedia defines friendship as:

'Value that is found in friendships is often the result of a friend demonstrating the following on a consistent basis:

− The tendency to desire what is best for the other

—Long-term friends are the people with whom we can reminisce about memories that occurred during our lifetime.

Brands will be able to recall every interaction we have with them throughout our lives. Companies and brands will be able to create a digital memory of their relationships with consumers. This will strengthen consumer trust in the brands they engage with. Creating relationships over the time based on trust will improve customer's loyalty towards brands.

The aim of companies will remain as it is now: to please consumers according to their needs. Companies will start gathering and storing large amount of data from users on their interests and preferences. Companies will have to compete among themselves in how effectively they are able to use this information. This information will be more objective and accurate than the data gathered today. Companies will no longer depend on the analysis of customer satisfaction surveys, focus groups, polls and loyalty cards but receive reliable personal data from each consumer. Market research will become the marketing analysis of customer insights.

Data gathering and analysis create new possibilities for engagement with consumers. Brands will have a new way to appeal to consumers, by enabling them to get to know themselves better on the basis of generated data. The need to feel a sense of belonging to a group, tribe or brand could now be based on real consumer data. Brands will be able to compare users' behaviour and target potential consumers with similar behaviour to current consumers.

Data analysis also helps to define brands. With a greater understanding of its consumers, a brand would be able to refine its image to better appeal to them and promote the observed values of the group. The way that a brand would change its image would depend on whether the consumer base is demographically heterogeneous: i.e: race, age, gender, studies, politics or homogeneous. Using accurate data on consumers, a brand's image could be developed to reflect their personalities and preferences.

All this would be possible through the collection and analysis of data. The difference between the data that companies will start to have access to and the data currently analyzed are:

— **Accuracy**: it will be the customer who decides to share data with a company they are interested in.

— **Diversity**: data will come from everywhere, from the consumers brands are aware of and those they aren't

— **Real-time**: today a user's status might say that she likes the iPad, tomorrow it might say she hate it. From being right wing to becoming a Buddhist, brands will be able to keep up with the changing consumer preferences in real-time.

There is a new challenge to be faced by brands. Previously brands have sought out customers, asking them to be part of their tribe. With new technology, brands will find consumers who want to belong to their tribe according to their behaviour and their rules. Will brands be able to respond to the demand of these consumers? Whatever the case, there is still an opportunity to get to know consumers better and to be better able to satisfy their needs.

Chapter IX

Summary

Throughout this book, it has been demonstrated that it is much harder for an Internet user to forget than before. New technologies allow everyone to store much more information about their experiences and their lives on the Internet than ever before.

Online Behavioural Advertising has shown us how Internet companies are in control of storing information about our behaviour on the Internet. Their goal is to create behaviour profiles that match consumer's target behaviour. Countless companies and brands are willing to pay for this information to show their target consumers advertisments.

This book has outlined the companies, organisations and institutions that deal with the information generated daily by online users. The analysis showed how consumer organization in the United States and United Kingdom are trying to legislate the Internet Information Market to protect user's online privacy.

The research carried out illustrates that the user is not alone on the Internet. When a user opt-ins, sharing his behaviour, 13.1 companies tracked him throughout 100 blogs. They showed him over 80% more advertisements than those he would have seen if had opted-out.

Users are going through a learning process. News of data analysis and information gathered by online companies is reaching Internet users. More and more the online community recognises the benefits and dangers of sharing personal information with online companies.

Internet users are demanding the right to their personal data. Users want to be the owners of their digital information and to be able to decide what to do with it. From selling information to keep it private, users are now discovering that data is a commodity.

Digital Memory is a reality. We have seen how new technologies, research and applications are developing platforms that allow users to store information for future analysis and measurement to gain insights. The book considers the opportunities and possibilities a Wikipedia of human behaviour could gives society.

It is the dawn of a new relationship between companies and consumers. New technologies and the creation of information on the Internet are offering new opportunities to companies and consumers. There are new ways for companies to get to know their consumers better, creating a long lasting relationship based on trust.

Conclusion

New technologies allow the recollection of information on an unimaginable scale. While users are not yet able to take advantage of this information, companies in the business of online advertising are doing exactly that. The research highlights that engineers and scientists are not in contact with marketing specialists. When they develop algorithms and platform to offer advertisments to users, their goal seems to be to increase the revenue of publishers and advertisers. Satisfying the consumer in either the short term or the long term seems to be less of a priority.

It is shocking to see how after all these years of marketing, the accrued knowhow has meant nothing. While it is common knowledge that consumer satisfaction is the main key to success and that this was based on communication and trust, it was decided to do completely the opposite. Online companies have decided against starting an open dialogue with consumers about how they are gathering their information and what were they doing with it. This situation has generated a distrust of online companies among consumers.

During the development of this book, the author has thought that a Digital Memory would be more useful to companies than to consumers. Not only because of the insights that companies could obtain from consumer information but also because this would allow companies in the future to look back and learn from the mistakes they made. As has happened in the past, companies thought that the consumer was the product and they did not realize that consumers were the ones making business today and in the future possible.

As this book shows, finally we are entering the Golden Era of Marketing. Contrary to what many believe, anthropology, psychology, sociology and neuroscience are the basis of marketing. These are sciences based on observation, data gathering and individual analysis. There could not be a better moment to make marketing than now. It remains to be seen whether companies are prepared to face this new era. Fortunately, there are still millions of ways of satisfying consumers that are yet to be discovered. Now is when companies are going to start to get to know their consumers.

The author only hopes that this time, what has been learned will not get lost in Oblivion.

Appendices

APPENDIX A

Browsing History Google Chrome

1. Feb 29, 2012

Richard Davidson - Wikipedia, the free encyclopedia

en.wikipedia.org

Richard Davidson From Wikipedia, the free encyclopedia For other people named Ric ... ... d content Current events Random article Donate to Wikipedia Interaction Help About Wikipedia Community portal Recent changes Contact

2. Feb 29, 2012

ebay - Yahoo! Search Results

uk.search.yahoo.com

CNET - 29 Feb 01:14 More Ebay Headlines eBay - Wikipedia, the free encyclopedia eBay Inc. (NASDAQ: EBAY) i ... ... tion and shopping website in which people and ... en.wikipedia.org/wiki/EBay - Cached eBay - The World's Online Mark ...

3.Feb 29, 2012

amazon uk - Yahoo! Search Results

uk.search.yahoo.com

amazon.unbeatable.co.uk - Cached Amazon.com - Wikipedia, the free encyclopedia Currently (Nov. 2011) edit ... ... k by old reviews of the old translation, many ... en.wikipedia.org/wiki/Amazon.com - Cached Best Amazon UK Offers & ...

4.Feb 29, 2012

fussball - Google Search

www.google.co.uk

Fußball - Ergebnisse - 2. Bundesliga Fussball - Wikipedia, the free encyclopedia en.wikipedia.org/wiki/Fussball Fußball (also spelled Fussball, if ... ... ootball • Table football ... Fußball-Bundesliga - Wikipedia, the free encyclopedia

5.Feb 29, 2012

i wont give us - Google Search

www.google.co.uk

see this track getting some ... I Won't Give Up - Wikipedia, the free encyclopediaen.wikipedia.org/wiki/I_Won't_Give_Up "I Won't Give Up" is a song ...

6. Feb 29, 2012

neurociencia cognitiva - Google Search

www.google.co.uk

Search Results Neurociencia cognitiva - Wikipedia, la enciclopedia libre es.wikipedia.org/wiki/Neurociencia_cognitiva - Translate this page ... ... ciencia - Algunos temas de la ... Neurociencia - Wikipedia, la enciclopedia libre es.

7.Feb 29, 2012

phd neurociencia barcelona - Buscar con Google

www.google.es

Opciones de búsqueda La Web Páginas en español Páginas de España Páginas extranjeras tra ... ... Neurociencia. 1974 – 1979. Licenciatura Farmacia en Francia, MBA en Francia, 15 meses Profesor visitante de Penn Univ

8.Feb 29, 2012

emotive - Google Search

www.google.co.uk

the emotive issue of gun ... eMOTIVe (album) - Wikipedia, the free encyclopediaen.wikipedia.org/wiki/EMOTIVe_(album) eMOTIVe is the third album b ... ... tive Behaviour Therapy (REBT): Home ... www.arebt.org/ 14 Dec 2010 – Training courses, conferences, art ...

9. Feb 29, 2012

lloyds tsb - Yahoo! Search Results

uk.search.yahoo.com

More results from lloydstsb.com » Lloyds TSB - Wikipedia, the free encyclopedia History|Services|Dropping ... ... stablished in Birmingham, England in 1765 and ... en.wikipedia.org/wiki/Lloydstsb - Cached

10. Feb 29, 2012

Clickjacking - Wikipedia, the free encyclopedia

en.wikipedia.org

Feb 29, 2012. Find out more. Clickjacking From Wikipedia, the free encyclopedia Clickjacking (User Interfa ... ... witter's "Don't Click" prank, explained (dsandler.org)". Retrieved 2009-12-28. ^ Krzysztof Kotowicz (20 ...

11.Feb 29, 2012

moonrise kingdom - YouTube

www.youtube.com

2012 directed by Oscar Winner Sam Mendes. en.wikipedia.org 8. "Moon... by TheDailyConversation | 2,716 views ...

12. Feb 29, 2012

book pyscology memory - Google Search

www.google.co.uk

Psychology and Cognitive Neuroscience/Memory ... en.wikibooks.org/wiki/Cognitive_Psychology_and.../Memory Cognitive ... ... he_psychology_of_memory.html?id=RTp- ... Memory - Wikipedia, the free encyclopedia

13. Feb 29, 2012

Mediterranean diet - Wikipedia, the free encyclopedia

en.wikipedia.org

Mediterranean diet From Wikipedia, the free encyclopedia This article is about the ... ... de (http://www.who.int/chp/chronic_disease_report/en/.). Cardiovascular morbidity in patients with T2D ...

14.Feb 29, 2012

Tennis Partner in London | All Classifieds | Gumtree.com

www.gumtree.com

ofiles. Join Now! Date added Today, Wednesday 29th Feb tennis partner in east london.4 hours ago East Lo ...

15.Feb 29, 2012

Social Neuroscience: People Thinking About Thinking People: Amazon.co.uk: John T. Cacioppo, Penny S. Visser, Cynthia L. Pickett: 9780262517270: Books

www.amazon.co.uk

Want guaranteed delivery by Wednesday, Feb 29? Order it in the next , and choose Express deli ...

16. Feb 29, 2012

recipe yellow lentils - Google Search

www.google.co.uk

From Sunset Magazine March 2006. Awaken your ... Yellow Lentils Recipes reci ...

17. Feb 29, 2012

peeps - English-Spanish Dictionary - WordReference.com

www.wordreference.com

WordReference.com | Online Language Dictionaries English-Spanis ... ... s, meanings and examples. WR Random Word:

18.Feb 29, 2012

Facebook

www.facebook.com

On Oakley Sunglasses Compare Offers Today & Save! Facebook © 2012 English (UK) • Privacy • Terms • More Upda ... ... minutes ago • Like • 1 Edit options More stories Facebook © 2012 • English (UK) About • Advertising

APPENDIX B

Google Ads Preferences categories

Top-level categories

Animals
Arts and Humanities
Automotive
Beauty and Personal Care
Business
Computers and Electronics
Entertainment
Finance and Insurance
Food and Drink
Games
Home and Garden
Industries
Internet
Lifestyles
Local
News and Current Events
Photo and Video
Real Estate
Recreation
Reference
Science
Shopping
Social Networks and Online Communities
Society
Sports
Telecommunications

Travel

Subcategories of Entertainment

Entertainment!Celebrities
Entertainment!Clubs and Nightlife
Entertainment!Comics and Animation
Entertainment ! Comics and Animation ! Anime and Manga
Entertainment ! Comics and Animation ! Cartoons
Entertainment ! Comics and Animation ! Comics
Entertainment!Dancing
Entertainment!Entertainment Industry
Entertainment!Fashion and Modeling
Entertainment!Fun and Trivia
Entertainment!Humor and Bizarre

Entertainment!Humor and
Bizarre !Bizarre
Entertainment!Humor and
Bizarre !Humor
Entertainment ! Humor and
Bizarre ! Paranormal
Entertainment!Movies
Entertainment ! Movies !
Bollywood and
Lollywood
Entertainment!Movies!Horr
or Films
Entertainment ! Movies !
Movie Memorabilia
Entertainment ! Movies !
Movie Rentals and

Sales
Entertainment ! Movies !
Science Fiction
and Fantasy Films
Entertainment!Multimedia
Content
Entertainment ! Multimedia
Content ! Flash
Content
Entertainment ! Multimedia
Content !
Podcasting
Entertainment ! Multimedia
Content ! Video
Clips and Movie Downloads

APPENDIX C

Average PPC Costs

Metric	2005	2006	2007	2008	2009	2010	2011
Cost per click (CPC)	$0.38	$0.32	$0.62	$0.71	$1.03	$1.24	$1.04
Click through rate (CTR)	1.5%	0.7%	0.3%	0.3%	0.3%	0.7%	0.4%
Average Ad Position	4.0	4.0	3.9	4.0	3.6	3.7	3.0
Cost per mille (CPM)	$5.56	$2.38	$1.95	$2.16	$3.34	$8.55	$3.97
Conversion rate	3.8%	4.0%	7.0%	7.5%	6.0%	6.8%	5.3%
Cost per conversion	$10.18	$7.63	$6.41	$7.02	$12.60	$13.14	$19.74
Invalid click rate	n/a	3.5%	6.5%	4.9%	5.5%	6.7%	10.9%

APPENDIX D

What's Your Personal Data Worth?

Revealed Value of Personal Data

Your social security number / government ID	$240
Credit card information	$150
Digital communication history (chat logs, text messages, emails)	$59
Web search history	$57
Physical location history (your phone or car GPS records)	$55
Web browsing history	$52
Health history (medical records, diet, health routines)	$38
Online advertising click history	$5.7
Online purchasing history	$5.7
Social Profile (hobbies, interests, religious and political views)	$4.6
Contact information (phone number, email or mailing address)	$4.2
Demographic information	$3.0

US$/Year, median value, n=180

http://designmind.frogdesign.com/blog/what039s-your-personal-data-worth.html

References

Acquisti, A. (2010). *The Economics of Personal Data and the Economics of Privacy.* OECD Conference Centre, Joint WPISP-WPIE Roundtable. Carnegie Mellon University.

Alberts, D.S., Garstka, J.J., Hayes, R.E., Signori, D.A. (2001). *Understanding information age warfare.* United States: CCRP.

Anton, A.I., Earp, J.B., Young, J.D. (2010). *How Internet Users' Privacy Concerns Have Evolved Since 2002.* IEEE Security & Privacy, 8(1), pp. 21-27.

Asur, Sitaram and Huberman, B.A (2010). *Predicting the Future with Social Media.* HP Labs.

Baddeley , A.D. (2004). *The Psychology of Memory.* The Essential Handbook of Memory Disorders for Clinicians.University of York: John Wiley & Sons.

Benevenuto, F., Rodrigues, T., Cha, M., Almeida, A. (2009). *Characterizing User Behavior in Online Social Networks.* In Proceedings of the ACM/USENIX Internet Measurement Conference (IMC), Chicago, USA.

Chandon, P. and Morwitz, V.G. (2008). *Breaking Behavior Repetition: New Insights on the Role of Habits and Intentions.* Advances in Consumer Research, 126-128.

Chandon, P., Smith, R.J., Morwitz, V.G., Spangenberg, E.R. and Sprott, D.E. (2011). *When Does the Past Repeat Itself? The Interplay of Behavior Prediction and Personal Norms.* Journal of consumer research, vol. 38.

Chen, J., Stallaert, J. (2010). *Who welcomes Behavioural Targeting: An Economic Analysis.* Paper under review. University of Calgary and University of Connecticut.

Chen, Y., Pavlov, D., Canny, J.F. (2009). *Large-Scale Behavioral Targeting*. Proceedings of the 15th ACM SIGKDD Conference on Knowledge Discovery and Data Mining, Paris.

Cheung, C.M.K, Kwong, T., Chan, G.W.W. and Limayem, M. (2003). *Online Consumer Behavior: A Review and Agenda for future research*. Information Systems Department, City University of Hong Kong.

Clark, J.W., Tansey, R.R. and Wynn, G.W. (2004). *The planning fallacy: consumers' overly optimistic prediction of the future*. James Madison University and University of Alaska, Fairbanks.

Damasio, A. (2010). *Self Comes to Mind*. New York: Pantheon.

Dixon, P. (2007). *The Network Advertising Initiative: Failing at Consumer Protection and at Self-Regulation*. World Privacy Forum. Vol 15, p. 2009.

Dwyer, C. (2009). *Behavioral Targeting: A Case Study of Consumer Tracking on Levis.com*. Proceedings of the Fifteenth Americas Conference on Information Systems, San Francisco, California.

Foster, J.K. (2009). *Memory: A very short introduction*. New York: Oxford University Press

Foxall, G.R., Oliviera-Castro, J.M., James, V.K., Yani-de-Soriano, M. and Sigurdsson, V. (2006). *Consumer behavior analysis and social marketing: the case of environmental conservation*. Behavior and Social Issues, 15, 101-124.

Frith, D. (2007). *Make up the mind*. Oxford: Blackwell.

Hasson, U., Ghazanfar, A.A., Galantucci, B., Garrod, S., Keysers, C. (2012). Brain-to-brain coupling: a mechanism for creating and sharing a social world. *Trend in Cognitives Sciences*, 16,2, 114-121.

Ho, T.H., Lim, N., Camerer, F. (2006). *Modelling the psychology of consumer and firm behaviour with Behavioural economics*, Journal of Marketing Research: Vol. 43, No. 3, pp. 307-380.

House Rules Committee (2012). *The Cyber Intelligence Sharing and Protection Act*. Rules Committee Print 112-20.

Hsieh, N. and Chu, K. (2009). *Enhancing Consumer Behavior Analysis by Data Mining Techniques.* International Journal of Information and Management Sciences, 10, 39-53.

Janis, I.B. and Nock, M.K. (2008).*Behavioral Forecasts Do Not Improve the Prediction of Future Behavior: A Prospective Study of Self-Injury.* Harvard University, Journal of Clinical Psychology. 64,10 1-1.

Kensinger EA, Addis DR, & Atapattu RK (2011). Amygdala activity at encoding corresponds with memory vividness and with memory for select episodic details. *Neuropsychologia, 49,* 663-673.

Letouzé , P. and Oliveira, R.L. (2011). *Internet-Based Information Consumer Theory A Baudrillard's Perspective*. International Conference on Social Science and Humanity IPEDR vol.5.

Malhotra, K.N., Kim, S.S., Agarwal, J. (2004). *Internet user' information privacy concerns: the construct, the scale, and a causal model*. Information systems Research, 15,4, 336-355.

McDonald, A. and Cranor, L. (2008). *The Cost of Reading Privacy Policies*. I/S: A Journal of Law and Policy for the Information Society.

McGrew, W.C.(1998).*Culture in Nonhuman Primates?*. Annual Review of Anthropology 27: 323.

Paine Schofield, C.B., Stieger, S., Reips, U-R., Joinson, A.N. and Buchanan, T. (2007). *Internet users' perceptions of 'privacy concerns' and 'privacy actions'*. International Journal of Human-Computer Studies, 65, pp. 526 – 536.

Reitz, C., Brickman, A.M., Brown, T.R., Manly, J., DeCarli, C., Small, S.A., Mayeux, R., (2009). *Linking hippocampal structure and function to memory performance in an aging population.* Arch Neurol.66(11):1385-92.

Reyna, V.F., Chapman, S., Dougherty, M., Confrey, J. (2012) *The adolescent brain: Learning, reasoning, and decision making.* Washington DC: American Psychological Association.

Rich, J. and Smith, M. (2007). *Invasion of Privacy through internet monitoring.* Contemporary Ethics Taking.

Schacter, D. L., (1987). *Implicit memory: history and current status.* Journal of Experimental Psychology: Learning, Memory, and Cognition, 13, 501-518.

Siegel, D. (2009). *Pull: The Power of the Semantic Web to transform your business.* New York: Penguin Group.

Small, G.W, Moody, T.D, Siddarth, P. and Bookheimer, S.Y. (2009). *Your Brain on Google: Patterns of Cerebral Activation during Internet Searchin.* Am J Geriatr Psychiatry 17:2.

SoÈderlund, M. and Gunnarsson, Jonas (1999). *Predicting purchasing behavior on business-to-business markets.* European Journal of Marketing 35,1/2.

Stevens, G. (2011). *Privacy Protections for Personal Information Online.* Congresional Research Service. Prepared for Members and Committees of Congress.

Toubiana, V., Narayanan, A., Boneh, D., Nissenbaum, H., Barocas, S. (2010). *Adnostic: Privacy-Preserving Targeted Advertising.* NDSS.

Tulving, E., (2002). *Episodic memory: from mind to brain.* In: Annual review of psychology 53:1-25.

Visions of an industry, expert group (2009)*Future Internet 2020.* DG Information Society and Media Directorate for Converged Networks and Service –*"The Internet People".*

Yan, J., Liu, N., Wang, G., Zhang, W., Jiang, Y., Chen, Z.(2009). *How Much can Behavioral Targeting Help Online Advertising?* WWW, 261-270.

Electronic Sources

Alford, H. (2012, March).*Your Privacy Is Tested With Every Click You Make.* Retrieved April 29, 2012 from New York Times, http://www.nytimes.com/2012/04/22/fashion/your-privacy-is-tested-with-every-click-you-make.html?_r=1&pagewanted=all.

Arthur, C. (2012, February).*The end of online privacy?.* Retrieved April 29, 2012 from The Guardian, http://www.guardian.co.uk/technology/2012/feb/28/the-end-of-online-privacy?INTCMP=SRCH.

Barnett, E. (2009, 10 February 2009) *Teenagers 'spend an average of 31 hours online'.* Retrieved April 10, 2012, from The Telegraph, http://www.telegraph.co.uk/technology/4574792/Teenagers-spend-an-average-of-31-hours-online.html..

Cellan-Jones, R. (2012, January).*European Commission to reveal plans to change data privacy laws.* Retrieve April 29, 2012 from BBC http://www.bbc.co.uk/news/technology-16721542.

Cellan-Jones, R. (2012, January).*The battle over your data. Retrieved* April 29, 2012 from BBC, http://www.bbc.co.uk/news/technology-16732881.

Charlton, G. (2012, March) *82% of digital marketers think the EU cookie law is bad for the web.* Retrieved April 14, 2012 from E-consultancy, **http://econsultancy.com/uk/blog/9298-82-of-digital-marketers-think-the-eu-cookie-law-is-bad-for-the-web.**

Dailey, K. (2012, January).*Could Google's data hoarding be good for you?* BBC, http://www.bbc.co.uk/news/magazine-16749076.

Goodwin, D. (2012, 26 January*). New Google Privacy Policy Combines user data from all Google services.* Retrieved March 23, 2012, from searchenginewatch, http://searchenginewatch.com/article/2141451/New-Google-Privacy-Policy-Combines-User-Data-From-All-Google-Services.

Forden, S. (2012, February).*Obama Turns to Web Industry for Consumer Privacy Standard.* Retrieved April 29, 2012 from Bloomberg News,   http://www.bloomberg.com/news/2012-02-23/obama-looks-to-web-industry-for-online-consumer-privacy-standard.html.

Greeley, B. (2012, February).*The Consumer Privacy Bill of Rights: Are We the Consumers, Or Are We the Product.* Retrieved April 29, 2012 from Businessweek, http://www.businessweek.com/articles/2012-02-23/the-consumer-privacy-bill-of-rights-are-we-the-consumers-or-are-we-the-product.

Hochman, J. (2012). *The cost of Pay-per-click (PPC) Advertising-Trends and analysis.* Retrieved April 20, 2012, from Hochman Consultants, http://www.hochmanconsultants.com/articles/je-hochman-benchmark.shtml.

Kneller, M. (2012, April). *Impeding 'Cookie law' could mean £500k fine for businesses.* Retrieved May 1, 2012 from Talk business magazine, http://talkbusinessmagazine.co.uk/2012/05/bid-my-bill/.

Mark, J. (2011, November). European Study Reveals UK Internet Users Spend the Most Time Online. Retrieved April 10, 2012, from ispreview. http://www.ispreview.co.uk/story/2011/11/16/european-study-reveals-uk-Internet-users-spend-the-most-time-online.html

Pociask, S. (2012, March).*Stealing your privacy -- it's Google once again.* Retrieved April 29, 2012 from
 Foxnews, http://www.foxnews.com/opinion/2012/03/01/stealing-your-privacy-its-google-once-again/.

Sayer, P. (2012, March).*Yahoo says it will implement do-not-track worldwide later this year.* Retrieved April 29, 2012 from PC

Advisor,
http://www.pcadvisor.co.uk/news/security/3347920/yahoo-says-it-will-implement-do-not-track-worldwide-later-this-year/.

The Guardian (2012, March).*Privacy and the power of Google.* Retrieved April 29, 2012 from *The Guardian,* http://www.guardian.co.uk/technology/2012/mar/04/privacy-power-google?INTCMP=SRCH.

Lowe, A. (2012, March).*Google privacy changes 'in breach of EU law'.* Retrieved April 29, 2012 from BBC, http://www.bbc.co.uk/news/technology-17205754.

Scott, C. (2012, April) *Internet advertising revenue hit $31.7 billion in 2011.* Retrieved April 29, 2012, from Computer World Uk, http://www.computerworlduk.com/news/it-business/3352464/Internet-advertising-revenue-hit-317-billion-in-2011/.

Katz, I. (2012, April).*Tim Berners-Lee: demand your data from Google and Facebook.* Retrieved April 29, 2012 from The Guardian, http://www.guardian.co.uk/technology/2012/apr/18/tim-berners-lee-google-facebook.

Filloux, F. (2012, April).*Facebook's $100bn privacy dilemma.* Retrieved April 29, 2012 from The Guardian, http://www.guardian.co.uk/technology/blog/2012/apr/10/facebook-100bn-privacy-dilemma.

Sengupta, S. (2012, April).*European Regulator Warns Silicon Valley About Privacy.* Retrieved April 29, 2012 from New York Times, http://bits.blogs.nytimes.com/2012/04/26/european-regulator-warns-siliconvalley-about-privacy/.

Myers, R. (2012, May).*Giving up our liberty for free, one click at a time.* Retrieved May 15, 2012 from The Telegraph,

http://www.telegraph.co.uk/technology/facebook/9252949/Giv
ing-up-our-liberty-for-free-one-click-at-a-time.html.

Moules, J. (2012, May). *New 'cookies' rule loom.* Retrieved May
15, 2012 from *s* Financial Times,
http://search.ft.com/search?queryText=privacy.

Warman, M. (2012, April). *EU cookie law 'will cost businesses
£10billion'.* Retrieved May 1, 2012 from The
Telegraph,http://www.telegraph.co.uk/technology/Internet/92
23930/EU-cookie-law-will-cost-businesses-10billion.html.

Waugh, R. (2012, March).Google is now just an ad company':
Departing exec's Goldman Sachs-style rant about how search
giant is now obsessed with harvesting people's private
information. Retrieved April 29, 2012 from Dailymail,
http://www.dailymail.co.uk/sciencetech/article-
2115393/Google-ad-company-Departing-exec-James-
Whittakers-Goldman-Sachs-style-rant.html?ito=feeds-newsxml.

Wyatt, E, (9 May, 2012). F.T.C. and White House Push for Online
Privacy Laws. Retrieved May 15, 2012 from New York Times,
http://www.nytimes.com/2012/05/10/business/ftc-and-white-
house-push-for-online-privacy-laws.html

BBC News (2012, April*). Cyber-security bill Cispa passes US House.*
Retrieved April 29, 2012 from BBC,
http://www.bbc.co.uk/news/world-us-canada-17864539

Kennedy, J. (2011). *The personal information economy.*
Retrieved April 14, 2012 from Research,
http://www.research-live.com/features/the-personal-
information-economy/4006540.article.

Mahdawi, A. (2012, May). So you're an organ donor on
Facebook – but at what cost?. Retrieved May 5, 2012 from The
Guardian,

http://www.guardian.co.uk/commentisfree/2012/may/02/organ-donor-facebook-cost.

Heath, T. (2011). Web site helps people profit from information collected about them. Retrieved April 15, 2012 from The Washington Post, http://www.washingtonpost.com/business/economy/web-site-helps-people-profit-from-information-collected-about-them/2011/06/24/AGPgkRmH_story.html.

Information Age (2012). Personal data stores could be worth £1bn a year – report. Retrieved May1, 2012 from Information Age, http://www.information-age.com/channels/information-management/perspectives-and-trends/2100958/personal-data-stores-could-be-worth-1bn-a-year-report.thtml.

Condliffe, J. (2012). 'Social fMRI' app from MIT can predict its users' behavior. Retrieved March 19, 2012 from Wired, http://www.wired.co.uk/magazine/archive/2012/03/start/your-social-forecaster.

Malik, O. (2009). In 10 Years, Hours Spent on Internet Almost Doubled. Retrieved April 30, 2012, from Gigaom, http://gigaom.com/2009/12/24/1999-2009-hours-spent-on-internet-nearly-doubled/.

Hill, K (2012). *How Target figured out a teen girl was pregnant before her father did.* Retrieved March 4, 2012 from Forbes,http://www.forbes.com/sites/kashmirhill/2012/02/16/how-target-figured-out-a-teen-girl-was-pregnant-before-her-father-did

About

 J. Aranda Serralbo is an independent thinker, freelancer and self-proclaimed 'Digital Nomad'. Born in sunny Spain, he studied for a BSc Business and a BSc Human Resources Management at Pablo de Olavide Universtity in Seville. He took a MSc Marketing Research at Rey Juan Carlos University in Madrid and later on a MSc in Consumer Psychology at London Metropolitan.

Specializing in branding and human behaviour, he has experience as a product manager in a variety of fields. For the last two years he has worked within the behavioural department of Yahoo! as a Data Insight Analyst. He is one of the few to think that marketing must be devoted to promoting long lasting products and long lasting happiness.

He renounces the conventional '-isms' of the pre-Digital Age and promotes a professional life in which projects are developed online rather than in the office.

Currently you can find him travelling the world working as a freelance consumer psychologist and writer to satisfy his biggest hobby - problem solving. If you share his hobby, please don't hesitate to contact him to play together: javieraranda@outlook.com

www.ingramcontent.com/pod-product-compliance
Lightning Source LLC
Chambersburg PA
CBHW071244170526
45165CB00003B/1231